When the Moon Knows You're Wandering

Ruth Ellen Kocher

New Issues Poetry & Prose

A Green Rose Book

New Issues Poetry & Prose
The College of Arts and Sciences
Western Michigan University
Kalamazoo, Michigan 49008

Copyright © 2002 by Ruth Ellen Kocher. All rights reserved.
Printed in the United States of America

First Edition, 2002

ISBN: 1-930974-11-6 (paperbound)

Library of Congress Cataloging-in-Publication Data:
Kocher, Ruth Ellen
When the Moon Knows You're Wandering/Ruth Ellen Kocher
Library of Congress Catalog Card Number: 2001131164

Art Direction: Tricia Hennessy
Design: Joshua Clayton
Production: Paul Sizer
                 The Design Center, Department of Art
                 College of Fine Arts
                 Western Michigan University
Printing: Courier Corporation

When The Moon Knows Knows You're Wandering

Ruth Ellen Kocher

New Issues
WESTERN MICHIGAN UNIVERSITY

Also by Ruth Ellen Kocher

Desdemona's Fire

for Coby,
who finds me each time I lose direction

*O lovely stranger, sometimes in this place
we do not even allow the night to heal us.*

—James Wright

Contents

I. Lost and Leaving

Gustav's Arc	7
The Escape Artist	8
The Long Arm Forward	10
The Rapist's Birthday	11
The White Camel	12
Painting Apples	13
Another Letter Home	14
Sleepwalker on the Mountain	15
February Leaving	16
Drowning	17
He Dreams of Falling	18
Sestina Mouths the Object, the Word	20

II. Home

At Home the People Sing	25
Variable	28
Herself, in the Window	30
Lay Down Lilies	32
Stature	33
Taking Down the Ivy	34
The Wave Advances	35
When the Moon Knows You're Wandering	37

III. Wars Away

The Way Road	41
Ghost	42
Manifesto	44
A Man Begins His War	45
1944	46
The First Monsoon	47
Burial of a Boy from Across the River	49
The Hundred Coats	50

When the Moon Knows You're Wandering

I. Lost and Leaving

Who can know from the word goodbye
What kind of parting is in store for us

—Osip Mandelshtam

Gustav's Arc

The old man who rides his bike around the neighborhood
has finally come to take the cans away
down a road that leads to the rest
of this small city
dwarfed by large towns
to the west
which hug the earth's plate from the angry pacific fault
all the way to cliffs craning up from the sea.
The waves there move as if they had no more shore to hold,
nothing balancing the other hemisphere
that spreads in mountains knuckled
over the globe,
beneath an atmosphere paling in its own loneliness,
and too many miles away to comfort a raging Jupiter
once happy beyond the red eye of his storm
but now defeated and solemn, missing one
of the girls who's left him there,
one of his restless moons.

The Escape Artist

Of course you think of Houdini.
The dark chamber all around him
hollowed in water echo and the outward
heartbeat that takes up the whole space,
takes up your space and the envelope
of electric air above you. Forget him,
he is lost. He is the man in the dream
you never recognize.

Keep something for yourself.
The last breath. A flash of the woman
who sees you turn away when the lid
closes. There are reasons
to be delivered: the long road to the market,
a green carnival tent you've almost forgotten,
the tin, circular sound of a hub-cap
tracing the side of a road. Learn and remember
that the summer consumes us
even as we sleep and there is nothing
pure or exact or cruel in language.

There is more. There are taxi drivers
who search for their way by streetlights,
the women made-up into an evening
who laugh at a man who's passed them,
who can't find his way out of a crowded room—
and furthest away from even them, three boys
who've ridden their bikes down the street
holding summer's last terrible syllable. Are you
the voice that sends them
all into sleep, the someone in the dream
they do not know?

Now is the time to understand
the movement of your own
senses, the smell of mornings locked
into the memory of grass, butter burning,
purple garlic flowers shedding their last
pollen, the smell of wheat fields before
you see them. Soured milk. The rough

edge of lilac. You are waiting for the miracle?
You are waiting for the slim
left hand, for the right hand, fingers
that find their own way out of cool
confinement. You are free.

The Long Arm Forward

The night I dreamed a crane
draped in a gray sheet chased
my lover into the woods near our home,
the earth shook in Peru, covered a thousand
homes with mud and ash from a volcano
believed dormant. My lover was running silently away.
The crane was almost invisible under her sheet,
just the tip of flapping wings and long yellow legs.
In Peru, hands reach into rubble even now. The hands of dishes.
The hands of wood. Hands which are cold and warm,
sometimes wet. Hands that reach for a heavy hold,
that take us home, that speak somehow
and mold their forms into light like flocks of pale birds.
In this disaster, a woman remembers, a decade ago,
her husband drowning, and thinks,
through me you exist and fail. You
fail and exist again. Your mouth is full.
Leave me. Leave me alone.
She knows how easily lightning could erase her,
how the same water that carried
maroon legions of leaves past her home has changed
her life and the crane that haunts her sleep
so that it's not a crane, but a boy. A boy in a rain slicker
with muddy boots the color of mangoes
chasing storm through the woods until
he finds a stream. He is lost, and the woman . . .
I am lost and her husband lost and leaving.
Yes, I am sleeping on long yellow legs and hear
through rain the rumble of mountains,
very far away, their red floes steaming mud.
I hear a mountain waking this world.

The Rapist's Birthday

> *the wings of an angry swan*
> *can compass the earth*
> —H.D.

Today the mullein is five feet tall.
I'd forgotten about the cattails, the crown vetch,
the arborvitae jutting from the hedgerow
north of this field. I'd forgotten about
the skinned groundhog rotting in the stream
and how humid it was, even though the sun
broke through the canopy of trees. Until now.
Until I went to see our grandmother dying still
in a tiled room. She asked if I'd seen you.
She asked where her sister's gone and if I'd bring her
a piece of the candy her dead son bought ten years ago,
the deep-seated pangs of life still in her.
Today, the mailman dropped a package
while he fumbled through envelopes
bundled for the neighbor. Today
is someone else's birthday too. A girl
who broke her arm skating. A woman who hates
her husband because he loves his garden
more than her. The whisper of carrot.
The wild secret of yellow squash and strawberries.
On the other side of this mountain
a man stops to feed the rabbit caged behind his house
before joining his family, upstairs, for singing
and cake, and singing. In a week
he'll butcher the rabbit for a dinner of cheap merlot
and corn bread. But the animal will love him
as animals love, will wait for him to come
each of the next six mornings with celery
and lettuce, saying, eat well my friend.
I am sorry for you. Eat well.

The White Camel

> *No lie can live forever*
> —*Martin Luther King Jr.*

He leaves a road he's traveled
for thousands of years to look for me
in sullied places, the green heaped alleyways
between downtown shops, or the flatbeds of trucks
headed north in summer into the cool forgiveness
of Utah storms. Have you passed him on the highway,
like the notion you've forgotten something,
a shuffled blur you can't make out
hollow as the echo of a goatskin drum?
You may have seen him in the evening's first breath
under the yellow trumpet of cat's claw,
looking through a window where television
gave conversation to an otherwise quiet room.
His eyes are darker than mine. His lashes
brush long trails into the wind that float away
when he blinks, find a place in the palms as though
they've found home, again. You may have thought
he was a milk white crane bending to take a drink
from a stream, or a heron bowing his colorless throat
into flight, but he is not like that. He is my past
and he's lost his way. He'll trick you into telling him
where I am: whisper the sage secret of pine cones unraveling,
the tipped froth of ocean on his tongue, the weariness
of wind like his quiet voice of promises.
If he asks, tell him I am gone.
Tell him I am the pith of the last peach.
I am the movement you're just now forgetting.
Tell him the waves have taken my form.
That I am his past and I am lost also.

Painting Apples

Even in the lazy light of fall
we built a great effort into the air,
picking apples like so many ornaments
blown from the solid chill of October.
The orchards reached out
like not even you could, rows heading over each berm
directly west as if some path would find a home.
This morning,
while building my fire,
I could not help but think
of streets away from here, stone roads
in Edinburgh that crumple
with the will of moss finally finding light,
a farmer selling twisted oak
from a cart collapsing into its own
broken ribs, who might later tell his family
over broth and warm bread
of the American he'd seen
sobbing today, a grown man
letting salt frost in his beard. In this room
not even the walls will disclose
what we don't say about the color of apples
just before they drop, or the cold
easel screech, or the way
the smell of turpentine
soaks into everything.

Another Letter Home

The weather here stays cool. A policeman walks
past two boys sleeping in a doorway not far from me.

If they disappeared, he thinks, we would say prayers
like folds of African violets placed in the dark to bloom.

His hands are invisible to the boys, can do nothing for them.
There is no story to tell besides the policeman's prayers:

one for the boys, one for a girl. She has the terrible love of praying
mantis, this girl with short, short, dyed black hair, skin that's pale

because of the cold. I know her as the rumble of my lungs,
the dark morning which matters less to us than to the cop or the girl

who dyed her hair as her parents slept in a dream of their own,
matters less to us than to a woman who leads a goat over gravel

to a neighbor who trades for some chickens, a piglet.
Their hands have never touched me. I'm not even in their dreams.

I've learned from them I shouldn't have told you
about a moment in my life. I thought I could

and was wrong . . . thought a long moment, a man's
cruel weight, sour breath, single thought, could be forgotten.

The girl I pray for knows defeat is not a very large word
and that hands are always invisible, the stuff we make of them, the way

out of our beds in the morning. I stay here because the weather
is cool. Storms never break the ridge that frames

the valley beyond me. I thought ten years of not saying
could be disguised as the truth. When I pray,

I fold my hands tightly and think of the girl,
the sound of water turning black in her hands,

think of the hair flowing in water, and of the faucet,
and of her parents, sleeping.

Sleepwalker on the Mountain

And I search among the signs
For the flare, polestar, pulley toward the edge.
—Ruth Stone

Half back to consciousness
she begins her nocturnal, locked-eye search
for the same torment that lives in trees,
arms outstretched as if the route
were more apparent in the dark,
the mountain like her country
shivering its hulk of plenty.
She hears leaves begging for warmth,
finds her coldness, her surprised feet,
and the barrenness comes easily as trouble.
She is the plight of winter trees,
the screech of their thrown branches
scraping windows, the misery of driftwood
searching for a boulder,
and though the wind tries to make all things equal
the sleeper's hands pierce air,
reaching to have the curses of wood,
of mountain dirt, of trees.
Somehow in sleep
she envies the oak stump in her path,
vacant of sap and chilled to its memory
of root; the broken trunk
sits high on a hill of maple,
loneliest of things.

February Leaving

There was a thick summer.
There were cicadas and rows of grave markers,
mothers knitting and grandmothers
weaving their fading thoughts into combs of silver hair,
lightning bugs lost and flagging the woods,
homes that whispered to each other at midnight
the truth from their cellars.
I could say that none of this lives in us
because at night there are fewer hands
to wind the air into our pockets,
that bats are nervous in their temporary waking.
I can tell you that the grass sorrows
if there is no thunder or the earth shudders
where people sleep or the mountains mouth
their wishes silently into snow.

The truth is, in winter, the earth rejects us.

What do you say with memory—
that the continents long for each other
just as children who are bundled ghosts
leave their voices as trails in the woods,
that lakes are burdened with notions of ice
and heaviness, just like us.
The things we trust are less
and less true in winter.
I will say only that a cough
deep inside you
at the heart of your lung
will turn you around just in time
to see the rock cliffs you've dreamed of,
the bull seals searching
for beaches, for rocks that hold
the moss long, long into summer,
and a sun that's indifferent to the year,
to the herd, and to the ocean charging.

Drowning

It must have happened in the blue air
filtered into a summer night
so many years ago that no one
remembers
the green circle of algae
defining a pond's edge, an old boat
helpless against a steady rocking
that breathes a creak into her oars.
Every woman in my family
knows this fearful memory of water,
high weeds around the water shed,
a small perch,
backwards floating belly-up
in cattails,
the ancient drowning
stealing into each new year when the wet smell of growth
comes downstream
weaving moss and lichen out of rock.
No one remembers.
Evenings, in the shock of sun
that spills last over a valley, you can hear
voices calling to some
child stumbling near water
lost in the dizzying
revolutions of early years when blue coda
and colts-foot clutter smaller worlds in deep soil,
June bugs and cicada working their way
out of sleep,
into an almost suffocating wind,
suffering the deep churning of age.
Not a fear of water, but a knowledge
of the lives inside, of their grandmothers
who couldn't swim, and all the obedient daughters
with our discipline of stones.

He Dreams of Falling

At the table in patio seating,
a young man starched into my evening
in waiter black and white—
he's probably named John, Tom,
something less spectacular than the busboy
named Ari at the table beside me.
He is a boy I've seen and I hide that from him,
a silence he doesn't understand as he turns away
not remembering that a week ago while waiting for a bus
I saw him step over the legs of an old
homeless woman
sprawled on the sidewalk. His foot
not clearing her arm, caught,
so that he jerked her body
while a consciousness
almost found her but didn't,
just stirred somewhere below her face.
In the spiral where he turned he glanced
not at the woman but to see who'd seen.
He saw me watching him, jack-lighted and drawn
into the warm ceremony that fell through him.
I understood this explosion,
the burn from the beginning,
there when a bus passes, or a waiter
quietly puts down your check.
He could be my brother,
have parents at home in Ohio where there is a small lie
buried in a garden with snow peas and basil.
There may be another breaking the soil,
dogs who bark into the woods,
constellations who see our freeways as spines—
or he may miss a warm climate,
groves of oranges measuring the circular
scent of weight each time a heavy fruit falls.
He may know that secretly
the hearts of children conspire to stop
when parents close their bedroom doors.
But in this construction,
the pace that takes him back and forth
in the servitude of strangers,

he has forgotten, again, to feel for me,
eating alone, a woman familiar
deep in the eyes,
with his same knowledge of movement
that bends us forward,
the instinct of our heels
ready to turn against that jerk a body makes
even in dead sleep,
the stir that is less than we ask for,
less than an old woman,
or a woman growing old.

Sestina Mouths the Object, the Word

In my sister's room there is no tolerance for language
without regard for her tongue, which is hungriest for words.
She has a patience in emptiness reserved for the mouth,
and the thousand names of things, of not a thing she can say
but the word for itself, the overture of the object
that finds her speech. In my sister's room nothing finds a name—

not the too many hills, the many roads that all have names,
not nights when cows predicate their forms in damp earth, language
nothing for them, not heavy, dim or thick as the object
of grass, the smell of grass, blades of grass which need no words
for hunger to still be their hunger, though they never say.
Her window inhales and exhales rumors of twilight. It mouths

the consequences of morning into grids of sun. Mouth
of clouds. Mouth of rain, of bougainvillea. Lightning. Names
like telephone poles, crosses, martyrs whispering. They say
Joan. Theresa. Cecilia who said nothing, language
nothing for her but an endless braid of letters, of words
that her hands became. My sister is simple, the object

of her own dreams, of the dreams that become their own objects
and their own languages, of objects which are their own mouths
in her dreams of wood and gardens, radish, sweet carrot, words
of love leaving her mouth empty, searching for her own name,
leaving the words where the forest folds. Love leaving language
alone. My sister is the quiet beneath herself, says

more in her silences than silence is. She will not say
yes, it was you. She will not say yes, you are the object
I dreamed, the yellow face of someone familiar, language
of my long evening, the rowboat that was a painted mouth
on a dark lake searching for the two oars who had no names
but who were lovers, who left without even simple words

that would let them be found. My sister is the breath of words
that trail off into a blunt afternoon, of words that say
the color of peppers dried into heat, the name
of water moved in directions away from an object
that has broken the surface from above. She is the mouth
of a walnut that keeps inside itself secret language,

the form of words before the breath of form steals the object. My sister doesn't say. She mouths the word *never*. She mouths the nothing that is her name and sleeps tonight, her language.

II. Home

Appear on the shore of your dreams

—Frederico Garcia Lorca

At Home the People Sing

He who has not suffered under human bestiality
cannot become spirit
             — Kierkegaard

At home the people sing their grievings
out of the mud and into
the perfect angle of their doors.

This is a sure, sweet churn
of memory,

a small country
where three children carry snap beans
home to their father. The whole hot morning spent
chasing snakes and wrens from the tall grasses
              of their field, the sun
hard enough
to hurt them, their black,
black skin composing a thirst for songs
              to build a grief
that will stun the snakes, pucker
the beans, remember an exact width
of hallway before the first creaking board.

Even in this story
the wrens must call each other home.

At home, the people hum their yearnings
when summer sinks
into the low lit sky and every porch
on every street moves the same burden
of swings suspended
              with hope of weightlessness
and evenings chattered into remembrance.

Here is their July, a month of bazaars, when century
old bricks sweat the day back
into night air and the public square market

is green and fly-bitten and crates crack
from melons ripening while everyone
silently begs the wind to cut
the thick line of fermenting
fruit from their breath.

        This month
will always have a man in red pants
and a new blue shirt who bends on Water street to lace his shoes
then prays on one knee, his head hung so low
shoulder blades become wings
threatening to burst through his back

as though he believed and belief would carry him
high over this valley

Even without him
the Virgin will project herself
onto stucco or aluminum siding
like an image in water,
her blue robes
                breathing tears and a desire
for the whole ache of mourning
to navigate us home with a hunger
we can believe and keep.

Appalachians continue
to wear soft layers of moss
down to the rock teeth inside. The river
cuts deeper. Sky descends
in Atlantic storm.

                This is where the people sing,
far from me, where winters seem coldest
and the deep call of wilderness
screams through trees into the sore
landscape of quarry cliffs,
where woods turn suddenly into a city
of narrow roads
                and the old wander through town

searching for a doorway
to remind them their lives
                are not a pain they dream
to remind them they are alive.
These lives are where they sing.

Variable

He calls thinking I can help him
but because I can't concentrate, because I don't really listen
when people speak and I'm remembering my own life:

the nurse with the deep cleft who was in love
with the sound of trains, who let me brush
her long, brown hair—the medicine bottle in her hands,
confident she could calm me
in air that blued my nails cold:

I've thought of this
because he's called from a dark room to tell me
the cigarettes and the snow outside
remind him of me, that the cold
in his fingers reminds him of nights smoking
outside my home, my story of rhinoceros charging.

I imagine my nurse is there with him,
the room heavy with cigarettes he's smoked,
one after the other. He called to say he remembered
a man who hates him, who's somewhere
sipping coffee not understanding a wave of grief.
He listens for the familiar, the shape of my voice,
my hands, my shoulder, which he can't remember.

I know he could love the nurse I think of,
her confident face, the large oak in her dreams
burdened with grackles. But he wants something
to level him, tells me I smelled like snow,
nicotine, the last time we spoke, so I say
no, it was you. Yes, he says,
and I say, there's a train near my house
that has no schedule but shakes the bottles
on my windowsill when it passes, so that now
he knows I'm only a memory
and that somewhere a man remembers us both,
folds a newspaper under his arm and into his coat
pausing that moment before he pulls his collar closed
or that maybe a woman brushes her hair
and sees me at ten, coughing,

counting backwards to show off.
Between us all are lakes frozen into low sky,
orange-bellied southbound planes.
I'm torn, he says, without knowing
the division, the splintered,
the small reflections.

Herself, in the Window

A girl and a boy step into the birch woods:
a transposition of black and white
with low dark sky, culm bank hills bedded in leaves,
coal waste. Black slag. The absence of soil
for dust. The trees are white.
They do not understand
that the leaves are in love.

No. Begin again.

The boy is gone.
The song of miners is oil on the mud:
a long black slick puddled near birch,
a walk up the hill, water
rusted like the ore scraped earth.
Her neighbors are sleeping. Travelers
don't come to this town anymore.

I am the black girl and I'm remembering
how the snow crests turn dark in winter
so quickly as though the living have left this place
one by one—
their shoes still lined inside old doors
waiting for warm feet to want them again.
There are drawers filled with gloves piled like leaves
that twist towards some regretted direction.

This way. That way. Here.

She has found, after years, a season where the trees stop shedding
indifference that finds us as we sleep—
a place where language can rise from the dust cloud of a car,
or brittle sage purples an anger
long into the evening.

What does she ask—
that the clock forget itself,
her own iris in the window give back the pale boy
who climbed through yesterday looking for his dog,
the boy eclipsed by a car, by a man and his watch

and a streetlight blinking as though the road curved
out of boredom, out of landscape and vengeance . . .

Come back
to the beginning.

The ground is a black cloth
the white birch climb from. The real woods
died years ago. No matter how hard she looks
there isn't a song here. There are old mines
and white trees, another afternoon.
There's a room with a small bed the driver twists in
like a dog in his dream. He paddles his arms,
his legs. His eyebrows are twitching.
He sees a streetlight and the boy is gone.

Lay Down Lilies

The sun burned no harder than the moon
the evening we walked a mile to bury the blue fish
that had lived in the freshwater tank we'd bought for it.
The air split when it met our lungs,
swallowed and spewed in half seconds,
a visible breath that went its own way
as the smoke from burning houses departs
from the lives inside them.

I'd once buried a locket from a boy
who smelled like Fels-Naphtha soap
but who has no name in my memory,
and I'd buried a litter of hamsters that died
under my bed long before I knew him—
now this fish with its small brain
dead soft with parasites and wearing
death's humble gray would feed the earth again.

The flashlight beam found its way
in the dark as though it were home,
picking out the objects around us
as though they'd known
each other forever—
as if they were in love.
Out there in the dark on my knees,
smelling Fels-Naphtha and thinking
of my life under the rain
of thrown soil,
I was most alive
and most alive
I buried the dead.

Stature

We chose our path,
watched air-locks on the jugs for weeks.
Each escaped bubble of fermenting juice
seemed like a miracle finally let go.
Months before, I welted where blackberries grabbed me,
each spindled branch a claw protecting the fruit
ripened by July. We were impatient.
The whole ordeal made us vicious, untangling,
pillaging as if we were sent over three hills to slay,
to bring back small hearts of rivals,
pails of their wounds pressed for thin blood.
We found something most of the year,
lived the range until anything was ready to pick again
or the need to conquer eased out of us.
In your beard, the beard of a brother or father
smelling of Bear Meadow moss and pine sap,
I can see my figure moving through woods far ahead of you
as you think of a girl who isn't there yet
but already you know she speaks French in her sleep.
Her fingers are blunt with work.
In your beard your jaw-line has given away
the verdict of a season I'm already forgetting.
Our wine is sour and strong. Corrupted,
long before we breathed the story of wild vines,
their fading. The passing breath.

Taking Down the Ivy

Watching the day yawn
down into your garden, I find you
among all you've set to green, walls crawling above sprouting
thyme, marjoram, and statice seed.
You focus on the bougainvillea, tying back wiring vines
that spring with the young arc of small arms,
motion sending me
to photos of girls drowned in bogs
before their breasts became precious to anyone
or the keels of their hands had ever understood a woman's place
in her own body, the warm cove keen to growing things
as the soft soil where peasants might squat
to pull potatoes away from under foot.
I see the arms sweep thin rain,
circle back to catch a balance not meant for them
as they fall into the earth they become—dirt
that coughs them up in corn rows, their souls rising
for breath through any root,
any limb of mock orange sulking for sun.
Last night, you traced
the thin, keloid tissue on my neck
knowing the skin senses more there,
and all of the women you have
ever touched were with us,
the smoky hair of Sylvia who pleased you
best by mouth, the long hands that worked you
out of youth. Piloted into these blooms,
your hands are the hands of a man finding life
in quiet places, taking the ivy down with the solemn concern
of a groom, each graft set with the same intent
that ushers a stretch of growing.

The Wave Advances

Between the sidewalk
and the freeway circling our neighborhood,
the small area clogged with construction, heat,
ranch-style homes—I find four brown girls
like I once was: newly braided and twisted into their ribbons,
walking a dog and eating ice cream frozen to sticks—
      four girls who go on and on it seems, past
my house and the neighbor
and the mailboxes,

      on and on, and the dog with his head
hung in some animal desire that moves him forward,
panting the path in front of him. The dog is ugly,
too small and hunched. His nose is running and wet.
      The girls dress alike or attempt the same sneakers,
the same pink shorts, their T-shirts different only by bows
or butterflies or buttons so they're deep
in the world they make of this day.

      I can't imagine what girls think,
not even by lying, can't remember not even myself
lost in the evening's long summer, school over
and friends clinging to whatever path I chose.

      These girls, moving within
the circles of their braids, don't
see me, here, outside of them,
worried about the bougainvillea
whose growing weight will topple
the wall around my house, twenty-nine
concrete bricks piled at the feet
of who they know I am:

      I am the neighbor woman
who they're blind to. I am their mother
who doesn't look at them but asks
what they've done today
without knowing how impossible

a day is, how the morning
seems already so very far
and the evening is guesswork.
    I am the memory they'll look for
as they follow an impression of moments,
a path they've lost and then found—
that pushes them around so many dark corners,
back, eventually, to a world where
the constellations are not yet obvious.
I am old. I am the dog and I'm forgetting.

When the Moon Knows You're Wandering

The shadow slant of your own body
somehow takes the ground in,
desperately wanting the surface of grass,
rock of the familiar in the moon's eye:
light that blues your midnight form.
How many years have you been gone?
And who drove you away—not a man or a stone
seeming to mark some path you run towards,
but a wind that rose in the pink depth of your lung
like first breath, the exaltation in knowing

you are lost. Say your own name backwards to prove
you exist, an ancient tongue that steels the simple evening air on which
you rely like Pharoh building the tomb for years.

Know your old age already in youth as if you began
wrinkled and bent to the earth with old sorrows, cold hands.
You are not the field of wars that turn the earth over
and over like a thin coin, the girl suffering
ebola near a tree while her brother, coughing,
digs her grave. Go where you will.
The sun rises there. The water flows.
Women wake in the middle of the night
trying to remember their names, their faces.
The names of their fathers.
Keep this blue light near your heart,
the dull thunder of your want
tracing each step, each pace that seems like direction.
The moon knows you're wandering,
even though the road thinks you're home.

III. Wars Away

I did not come to solve anything.
I came here to sing . . .

—Pablo Neruda

The Way Road

Summer sometimes beats them here, slowed days lost,
heat. Their red sky. Heavy nights draping each bird's
territory. Flight. Their religious eating,
eating, eating and then
sleep comes to them slowly, within another wind,
not the movement carved in their hearts where hunger
lets less live. They fight, wind blown,
tearing sage brush blooms,
cat's claw, orange—stabbing the long and forward
flowers. Eating. Eating while sun breaks, falls cold,
ants trail off to larvae, fill a wren's death—
eating, eating more.
This is not a love poem, nor a simple breath.
Not breath, a hummingbird war, or story
of a failing sigh. It is wing fold, the birds' flight,
hunger under them.

Ghost

I came upon this boy
kneeling,
looking for a book.
His eye had been blackened
by some foot or fist
thrown in anger.
I wanted to take him,
there in the library,
hold his face in my hands,
his white warm milk cheeks,
Irish blush to the chin,
close enough so moisture
from his breath would gather
on my lips,
then
it was you in him, haunting
again. Your red hair,
your injured look,
bony knees pressed to the rug
sweeping me into
this cathartic sorrow,
wanting.

I'm not sure how you do this
to me. I barely remember you whole,
just the hair or beard,
the legs, arms, all separate,
never as one man who searched
desperately in the dark
for music without words
to make love to.

If you have passion
in your blood, if you remember
cold mud caked to our stomachs
as we floated two on a tube
at Turtle Pond,
burn your memory.
Forget the girl whose brown skin
startled you at first,

who didn't care for
making love to music
with or without words.
Breathe slowly and keep
your ghost beside you
when you think back to
the nights, black water,
Bach, our year.

Manifesto

A shadow grips a field heavy
as the hot hand of a lover. I witness the path light passes,
the death of clouds, barns, a boundary of old disputes,
the guidance of a berm near a dung pasture crawling in
to curdle the lung. I witness a boy. John or Jason or David
just come to love himself, his large hands first, the half circle
of his shoulders. Wild garlic speaks to him. *I am yours.*

Last night, I drank too much whiskey.
A girl died in my throat with a dozen
simple words: lotus, swan, sweetness, stir . . .

The boy touches his long adolescent
stomach, ripens against an even gravity. My vertigo.
The dove who heaves the moment baritone.

I am here. I am sick. I am sick of being
a woman, a curve in the chest that balances
the red secret of pomegranate against my lips,
my grinning half-moons, the sound of water raising
a sharp gust of circular breath that stuns me into his noon.
The hour turns us, frames the long fingers
schooled silver inside our stomachs,

each given to a separate tempered-hunger.
He touches the stretch of sternum, the low down of hair.
He touches the line that divides him in two.
He touches a recession of words in his chest.
He touches his mother who knows his scent.
He touches the ribbon of dung in the air.
He touches the welt of sweat on his skin,
touches the faithless movement he is.

A Man Begins His War

The crows *crack-ow* deep
into fields which have sprouted October
tassels of corn, calling my children
and wife into the attractive swells of an afternoon
meant for leaving. I make bread
like a starving man, impatient
with yeast and damp cloth covers
which keep the rising from its own
scaling, wheat-flecked skin,
knead
with the anger of widows who breathe
black gusts of stocking shrouds
and woven shawls until they are women
cloaked dark, both inside and out.
This is the war
of my sons, my uncles, of all boys
lying patiently in their beds waiting
for a long, red train to erupt from the countryside
and take them from the bright spackle of flowers,
the cracked brick siding, from black birds
crowing their wishes into a dim, deaf sky.

1944

Your ghost has filled the house
more completely than these rooms can stand.

Outside, our groves are burdened
with fruit frozen in mid-rot by hushed snow
and I know even you would be sad with the impatient halt of fall.

The milk truck that's been passing daily
has stopped its route now,
though we've cellar cheese enough till spring.
Those old women in town,
       who do not know the year is gone
look at us and nod their used faces as though this were their gift
to pass and the blue seal of cataracts dimming their eyes
is another gift taken,
       our children, their heart-clench,
like so many generous pains.

Follow the chapped sound of the screen
hitting the house in wind,
       the sharp lye rising
from soap cakes cut this morning. Come, some form.
Tell me anything. Find our room.

The First Monsoon

—for A.K.C.

Last week in Mostar, the fields were emptied.
The shot cows stiffened on their round backs,
balancing sky on the cleft angle of their hooves,
a sky that, all the while, sent clouds
into blue corners. This is not the story
of a woman in love or a girl who wakes beside herself
at 8:00 as the desert already enters her room.
Yes, a spine of ivy *does* rake the sun into splinters
that spell a name, then twists shadow into a girl,
but her mouth is dim and blind, comfortable
with closeness and being, full of her tongue.

The farmers killed outside of Travnik
did not know that today, in this hemisphere,
the first monsoon would tear
palm fronds into fringes while I heard you
breathe long vowels of mourning. I have lied again
to tell the story right. Imagine the limes which are green
but not ready to eat. The first fiber under the skin
could be stone, could be the gray promise of another
long season, the acacia already spent in heat,
the air waiting to break in thunder over the brown backs
of migrants who have caravaned up from the south.
They hang lanterns on their ladders, work the opal-deep dreams
of their children, filling baskets suspended on their hips,
remembering with one orange the smell of their grandmother's robe,
with another, the coffee for lunch, remembering words
swallowed with wafers, wine, with each orange layer
peeled back to fathers whose cigars were sweet smelling,
the lover whose name has drifted into another grove, the wife,
her hair rich with mines and lemon. They don't know
the high peaks of Alaska where the glaciers
recognize your posture, cold against the cliffs.
They don't know the day which has brought you here to my house,
to my peppers hanging and the piano holding my whole life
in frames with faces smiling as though they know

something we should know of the women leveled this week
in their gardens near fresh winter radish.

In a pond near Mostar, three geese have found
a way to live through the silence all around them.
They are waiting for the United Nations' trucks
to bring them corn and white bread sent from America.
They are waiting for summer, and the end of summer
when they will leave and wait to be found by an accident
of direction, by a fluctuation of wind that began
a hemisphere away, the order of their movement
started in a storm east of where they've never been.
These are your figures twisted into a mortem pose,
emerged from your touch on the counter, the glass,
the bowl that is clear, empty, around each of our names.

Burial of a Boy from Across the River

The sky burned white
into his gills, into a sad fold of sleep.
This creature, his cold fins,
wrapped our legs into that dusk
of the pond, left us
wanting another breath
beyond the barn and what we believed
a wilderness of what lives,
of cows grazing fields
caught in their own movement,
kindling fires and the night
thrown from our homes.

Whose hair spun light back at you?
A breath singed with sour milk.
Him, the boy who could save us.

I bury myself with books
in a long week of wheezing, another winter
hidden in. The fire hall sounds.
Across the river
a church is burning—
the empty hole where memory should live:
an old face, the face of a peasant,
a fry cook.

In our path you put the thick assurance of fog,
a pinpoint of trees, the curve of a ditch
coming around to greet us,
a small light revealing stones.
This time we will come, meet
where the dark lays us down, binds us
to the dry comfort of our hands.
We have no prayers but our own breath,
our tongues. We have no voice here.

The Hundred Coats

They know their lives, early and late, and set out
—Norman Dubie

I.
After the ground has swelled open,
cracked with some inner anger,
we have another earthquake aftermath
and the storms far north of here return to cold
even in pictures, not because of the sharp asphyxiation
of color and film but the stillness of frost and freezing,
the invisible paralysis and cold hand of water.
Everyday, I ask forgiveness for sins I've forgotten
but feel are constant while others fight,
sure of something. Even the ground
has betrayed us with so much to remember:

an old coat which was not warm
but made a woman forget the cold
long enough to go outside and see her breath
still coming out of her, to see the arborvitae
bend again to wind and years later
the fuchsia dry crackle of bougainvillea
dusting her feet. She does not understand
the meaning of languages, the leaves
which have grown into
large words and small words
blown together around the feet of strangers
who recognize each other but don't say hello,
the factions of those
who surround us like friends and family
in syllables of intimate combinations.

Her last word may be a rush of air
into her lungs and then a pulse forward,
anticipating the thin consistency of a photograph,
a flood, a volcano, more words from a lover
near the reflection in a car's fender of sky
or an irrigation ditch which carries
the smooth mud of August against her form
as she passes. She says to herself, *Where are you?*

II.
She knows of other continents, other lives
failing to slip from this pulse still knowing
the small space they hold beneath their ribs,
beneath the hands they eat with. Go closer.
You can see her form against the window,
shadowed even now as though you're forgetting.
At the same moment you see her, one hundred blue herons
have taken off for the place of their own memories,
or those of their parents, or theirs,
or a whisper from a gull into their sleeping nests
three thousand years ago. Beneath that flight,
a man in Chicago looks for the center of his house,
a place where he can walk a circle without stopping
to move the chair that's been framed to one body,
or the mahogany table, the place where the form
of one path will come back to itself, so he can forget,
finally, how he came here.

Go now. Go home and sit in the armchair that knows your body,
the sink you've looked into when looking away from yourself,
the thrift shop bed that holds your smell
in the singular way inanimate things come to love us
by giving us back some of ourselves.
Has the earth erupted again? Has it come into our lives
and rudely shaken us out to find the hundred coats
we've forgotten, to see ourselves distantly
remembered, just once more, movement
like wind and walking, flight and the path
we gain, we lose, we find, we lose?

Acknowledgments

The Missouri Review: "Drowning," "Gustav's Arc,"
"The First Monsoon," "The Long Arm Forward,"
"Variable," "February Leaving"
Willow Springs: "Sestina Mouths the Object, the Word"
Gettysburg Review: " At Home the People Sing"
Antioch: "1944"
Prairie Schooner: "Ghost"
Poet Lore: "Lay Down Lilies"
West Branch: "Stature" (appeared as "Blackberry Wine")

Thank you to the many readers who have tirelessly read and re-read many of the poems in this book, including Herb Scott. Thank you especially to Norman Dubie, Beckian Fritz Goldberg, Alberto Rios, Jeanneane Savard, Bruce Weigl, John Balaban, and John Haag, for both kind and harsh words, and to Amanda Coffey, Jorn Ake, Deirdre O'Connor, Mary Gannon, and Jeff Hardin for being long-time confidantes and lovers of verse.

Ruth Ellen Kocher is the author of *Desdemona's Fire* (Lotus Press, 1999), winner of the Naomi Long Madgett Poetry Award. She received her Ph.D. in literature and M.F.A. in Creative Writing from Arizona State University. Her work has appeared in *African American Review*, *The Gettysburg Review*, *Ploughshares*, *Antioch*, and *The Missouri Review*, among other journals, and has been translated into Persian in the Iranian literary magazine *She'r*. She currently lives in St. Louis, Missouri, and teaches literature and writing at Southern Illinois University, Edwardsville.

New Issues Poetry & Prose

Editor, Herbert Scott

James Armstrong, *Monument in a Summer Hat*
Michael Burkard, *Pennsylvania Collection Agency*
Anthony Butts, *Fifth Season*
Gladys Cardiff, *A Bare Unpainted Table*
Joseph Featherstone, *Brace's Cove*
Lisa Fishman, *The Deep Heart's Core Is a Suitcase*
Robert Grunst, *The Smallest Bird in North America*
Mark Halperin, *Time as Distance*
Myronn Hardy, *Approaching the Center*
Edward Haworth Hoeppner, *Rain Through High Windows*
Janet Kauffman, *Rot* (fiction)
Josie Kearns, *New Numbers*
Maurice Kilwein Guevara, *Autobiography of So-and-so: Poems in Prose*
Ruth Ellen Kocher, *When the Moon Knows You're Wandering*
Steve Langan, *Freezing*
Lance Larsen, *Erasable Walls*
David Dodd Lee, *Downsides of Fish Culture*
Deanne Lundin, *The Ginseng Hunter's Notebook*
Joy Manesiotis, *They Sing to Her Bones*
David Marlatt, *A Hog Slaughtering Woman*
Paula McLain, *Less of Her*
Sarah Messer, *Bandit Letters*
Malena Mörling, *Ocean Avenue*
Julie Moulds, *The Woman with a Cubed Head*
Marsha de la O, *Black Hope*
C. Mikal Oness, *Water Becomes Bone*
Elizabeth Powell, *The Republic of Self*
Margaret Rabb, *Granite Dives*
Rebecca Reynolds, *Daughter of the Hangnail*
Martha Rhodes, *Perfect Disappearance*
Beth Roberts, *Brief Moral History in Blue*
John Rybicki, *Traveling at High Speeds*
Mary Ann Samyn, *Inside the Yellow Dress*
Mark Scott, *Tactile Values*
Diane Seuss-Brakeman, *It Blows You Hollow*

Marc Sheehan, *Greatest Hits*
Sarah Jane Smith, *No Thanks- and other stories* (fiction)
Phillip Sterling, *Mutual Shores*
Angela Sorby, *Distance Learning*
Russell Thorburn, *Approximate Desire*
Robert VanderMolen, *Breath*
Martin Walls, *Small Human Detail in Care of National Trust*
Patricia Jabbeh Wesley, *Before the Palm Could Bloom:
    Poems of Africa*